easter eggs

easter eggs

40 Fabulous Projects for the Whole Family

projects and photographs by

Matthew Mead

CHRONICLE BOOKS

SAN FRANCISCO

Library of Congress Cataloging-in-Publication Data available.
ISBN-10: 0-8118-5943-6
ISBN-13: 978-0-8118-5943-1
Manufactured in China

Distributed in Canada by Raincoast Books
9050 Shaughnessy Street
Vancouver, British Columbia
V6P 6E5

10 9 8 7 6 5 4 3 2 1

Chronicle Books LLC
680 Second Street
San Francisco, California, 94107
www.chroniclebooks.com

Produced by Downtown Bookworks Inc.
President Julie Merberg   **Senior Vice President** Pam Abrams
Editor Sara Newberry   **Design** Emily Waters   **Text** Carol Spier
Special thanks Patty Brown, Dinah Dunn, Sarah Parvis
www.downtownbookworks.com

Aleene's Tacky Glue is a registered trademark of Aleene's Licensing Co., LLC. Dremel is a registered trademark of the
Credo Technology Corp. Mod Podge is a registered trademark of Plaid Enterprises Inc. Mylar is a registered
trademark of DuPont Teijin Films. Styrofoam is a registered trademark of the Dow Chemical Co.

Notice: This book is intended as an educational and informational guide. With any craft project, check product
labels to make sure that the materials you use are safe and nontoxic. "Nontoxic" is a description
given to any substance that does not give off dangerous fumes or harmful ingredients
(such as chemicals or poisons) in amounts that could endanger a person's health.

Acknowledgments
Thank you to everyone who contributed to the creation of this book and helped to "hatch"
all of these projects. I would especially like to thank Pam Abrams and everyone at
Downtown Bookworks, Carol Spier, Lisa Bisson, Sue Chandler, and all the creative
editors at Chronicle Books. Special thanks to my wife, Jenny, who keeps me
grounded and organized, and Lisa Smith Renauld, our craftsperson
extraordinaire, without whom all our intricate and detailed
crafts projects would not be possible.
—Matthew Mead

simple ● moderate ●● advanced ●●●

introduction

FOR AN EVEN COAT OF PAINT on a blown egg, use a skewer to hold the egg while you're painting it, then stand it up on a foam pad to air-dry.

The egg is a symbol of spring and renewal, a source of life and nourishment, and, for creative people, it's a perfectly shaped blank canvas just waiting to be colored, decorated, and displayed as part of our seasonal celebrations.

Egg decorating is a traditional and treasured part of my family's Easter preparations, so creating the 40 projects in this book was an occasion of great fun at the Matthew Mead studio. Whether you share this activity with children or friends, or enjoy working alone to create gifts or holiday displays, we think you'll find many fresh, pretty, and charming ideas here to craft and treasure. We wish you a happy egg-decorating experience—a time of memories in the making.

Get off to a good start

This book begins with an overview of egg-decorating techniques—from how to blow an egg to the kind of gear you need to handle the eggs while you dye, paint, cut, and decorate them.

The projects range from simple to advanced. Each project has a skill-level icon—one egg indicates simple to do, two eggs indicate moderate difficulty, and projects with three eggs are the most challenging. The icons are there to give you an idea of what's involved; one person's challenge is a snap to someone else, and vice versa. We encourage you to try the projects that appeal to you even if you're not experienced with a particular technique. These are only eggshells, after all, so your first try can be called a practice piece if it doesn't turn out quite as you wish.

Choose your eggs

Most projects may be done using any size egg; however, the larger the egg, the easier it will be to handle while decorating and the greater the impact of the design will be. Unless noted, the eggs we've used are size extra-large. If you are going to paint the eggs with acrylic paints, which are opaque, it doesn't matter whether they are naturally white or brown. If you are going to dye them or paint them with watercolors, they should be white.

Many egg decorating projects can be done with either hard-boiled or blown eggs. Hard-boiled eggs are easier to dye, because they sink by themselves; blown eggs must be held down until they fill with dye or they will float on top of the dye bath. But hard-boiled eggs won't keep for a prolonged time and should be refrigerated until you are ready to display and eat them.

Organize your gear

The directions for each project in this book list the materials and tools needed under the heading "gather." Common household items such as pencils and scissors are not listed unless a specific type or size is required. It's a good idea to have basic crafts supplies handy when you're working—you never know when you'll have a great idea for putting your own spin on a project and want to use something not on our list! Below are tools and materials we use often. There is a handy resource list on page 95.

DECOUPAGE MEDIUM (Mod Podge is one brand) is used to adhere paper and small embellishments to the eggshell. Also important is a quick-setting craft glue such as Aleene's Tacky Glue or a glue gun with glue stick. (Where would the craftsperson be without this piece of equipment!)

A TAPESTRY NEEDLE is the perfect tool for piercing an eggshell and also for threading yarn or twine through an empty eggshell.

A DREMEL DRILL (found at art-supply stores, see Resources, page 95) with a mandrel bit fitted with a cut-off wheel can be used to cut the eggshells straight across.

ACRYLIC CRAFT PAINT works well to base coat an egg or paint patterns on it. These paints come in 2-ounce containers, perfect for egg decorating.

WATERCOLOR PAINTS, CHALK, CRAYONS, AND PERMANENT MARKERS with various point thicknesses are all good for making decorative patterns on the eggs. White crayon acts as a resist to egg dye, and can be used to make pretty batik designs.

NEEDLE-NOSE PLIERS are invaluable when you need to chip away bits of eggshell to create large holes or for open-egg projects.

PAINTBRUSHES. You'll need small ones, both bristle and foam. Flat ones are good for painting an entire egg and for applying decoupage medium and glue. Round ones and liner brushes (with long, pointed bristles) are better for small details and lines.

WOODEN SKEWERS in a couple of lengths are a must—for breaking up the egg contents so you can blow out the shell easily, for supporting the empty shells when you paint them or as they are drying, and for helping to manipulate decorations on the shells.

A CRAFT KNIFE (such as an X-acto), a mat knife, and a variety of scissors or small shears will come in handy for cutting paper and trimmings.

LONG TWEEZERS help you hold, place, or manipulate small embellishments.

A DREMEL DRILL with a mandrel bit and a cut-off wheel makes it possible to cut straight lines in blown eggs.

WHITE CRAYON acts as a resist to egg dye making it perfect for batik designs.

The easy way to blow an egg

Here's a great way to blow eggs that is efficient, sanitary, and creates no mess. To begin, gather the following:

Eggs in an egg carton
Straight pin or tapestry needle
Teaspoon (from your silverware, not for measuring)
Wooden skewer
Drinking glass
Drinking straws

Leave the eggs in the carton while you pierce them. Place the pin point-down against the top of the egg and lightly tap the pin head with the back of the spoon until it pierces the egg. Insert the wooden skewer into the egg and gently press it down until it pierces the bottom of the egg.

Remove the egg from the carton, hold it over the glass, and push the skewer up and down through the contents several times to break the yolk. Remove the skewer and place a straw over the hole. Blow through the straw until the contents of the egg are emptied into the glass. Rinse blown eggs in warm water and dry with a paper towel or let them dry in a clean egg carton.

Clean and dry the eggs before coloring

Gently wash the inside and outside of the empty eggshells with dishwashing detergent and rinse them. If water remains inside an egg, use a straw to blow it out. Let the eggs dry thoroughly on a rack (see page 10) or in their carton.

Sterilize eggs to be filled with edibles

If the eggs are to be filled with candies, sterilize them instead of just washing. Fill a saucepan with water. Place the blown eggs in the water one at a time, holding each one down until it fills with water and stays submerged. Make sure the eggs are covered with water. Bring the water to a boil and simmer, uncovered, for 15 minutes. Remove the eggs to a drying rack and let them drain as much as possible. When they are cool enough to handle, drain any remaining water by blowing it out with a straw.

Submerge the eggs in a bowl of cool water and then drain again. Transfer them to an egg carton and let stand at room temperature to dry.

Techniques at a glance

Dyeing

Mix commercial dyes according to the package directions. Submerge the egg in the dye—use the wire dipper or a spoon to hold down a blown egg until it fills with dye. Leave the egg in the dye for 20 minutes. Use the dipper or spoon to remove the egg and drain it on a paper towel or in a carton. For eggs meant to be eaten, you can also use food coloring or specially made food-grade egg dyes. Or you can find recipes online to make your own natural dyes from herbs, spices, vegetables, and other edible products.

Painting

TO BASE COAT AN EGG place it on a skewer, angling so the top of the skewer supports the egg. Use a small flat paintbrush to cover the entire surface of the egg with paint. Insert the skewer in the Styrofoam drying rack and allow the paint to dry completely—this usually takes about 5 minutes.

TO HAND PAINT DETAILS ON AN EGG, use a liner brush. Dip it in paint, place it on the egg, and bear down gently to begin the stroke; as you complete the stroke, decrease the pressure to make the line thinner. Lift the brush. You may want to practice this on paper first.

TO STENCIL AN EGG, place the stencil where you want it and hold with the fingers of your non-painting hand. Dip a stencil brush into paint, brush off most of the paint onto a paper towel. With a small circular motion, move the brush over the open area of the stencil.

TO SPATTER-PAINT, first dilute the paint with water and, if you wish, cover your worktable with newspaper. Slide the egg onto a skewer on a drying rack. Dip a stiff, flat brush in the paint, hold it in one hand above the egg and run your thumb along the bristles or tap the handle to create a spray of paint. Revolve the egg to spatter the surface as desired.

TO PAINT DOTS, dip the end of a paintbrush handle into paint and press it gently onto the egg. One dip will usually make a couple of dots.

HARD-BOILED OR BLOWN EGGS can be colored with commercial dyes. Remove eggs with a wire dipper or slotted spoon after 20 minutes.

SPATTER-PAINTING EGGS (below left) works best when you use a stiff, flat brush. Painted dots (below right) can be easily applied with the handle of a small paintbrush.

TO DECORATE YOUR EGG, consider embellishments intended for scrapbooking, jewelry-making, or clothing design.

SKEWERS AND STYROFOAM are all you need to make drying racks. The horizontal rack (below left) allows you to nest eggs while painting or gluing on details; the vertical rack (below right) is excellent for drying just-painted eggs.

Enlarging a hole

Hold the egg in one hand, and with the other, use small needle-nose pliers to gently chip away the shell around the hole. You can also break the shell between your finges.

Placing embellishments

Hold the egg in one hand or nest it on a drying rack. Apply glue where you want the embellishment and use long tweezers to hold and position the embellishment.

Piercing a design

Place the egg on a padded surface. Tap the eye end of a tapestry needle gently with a hammer until the needle pierces the shell. Experiment with different size needles. The more holes you pierce, the more fragile the egg becomes, so be careful.

Cutting the shell

A Dremel drill with a mandrel bit fitted with a cut-off wheel will cut a shell to create a cup or slit for inserting a card. Draw a line around the egg wherever you wish to cut the shell. Hold the egg in your non-cutting hand. Turn on the drill and place the wheel on the drawn line. Turn the egg under the wheel to cut along the line.

Set up racks for drying and decorating

Rack for horizontal drying

You can use this rack to support eggs while you are applying embellishments or painting details. Cut the skewers into 7-inch lengths. Insert them into the foam base, spacing them about 1 inch apart. Gently lay the eggs on top of the skewers. You can vary the skewer height and angle to make a little nest for each egg.

Rack for vertical drying

This rack provides the best support for wet painted eggs. Cut the skewers into 7-inch lengths. Insert them into the foam base, spacing them 2 to 3 inches apart so you can support a blown egg on each without the eggs touching. To use the rack, remove the skewers, insert each into an egg, angling the egg a bit so the top of the skewer supports the shell and doesn't go through the top hole, paint the egg, and then reinsert the skewer into the foam.

Egg cartons are good for drying, too

To dry washed or dyed eggs (which are colorfast when they come out of the dye bath, and won't smudge) simply place them in an egg carton.

EGG CUPS, salt wells, juice and cordial glasses, and small vases are some of the vessels you might use to display your finished eggs.

Have good trimmings at the ready

Choosing and using embellishments is half the fun of egg decorating. If you don't already have a stash of of trimmings, you can find myriad options at crafts supply, cake decorating, and fabric stores—with lots of goodies available online, too (see Resources, page 95). Some of our favorite trimmings:

SEQUINS, TINY MARBLES (little beads without holes), and GLITTER all add sparkle.

RIBBONS and CLOTH FLOWERS are fun to add to the eggs themselves and also good for dressing up containers and giftwraps.

SCRAPBOOK EMBELLISHMENTS come in many shapes and colors; they'll add instant graphics to your eggs.

TRANSFER OR PRESS-ON LETTERS make personalizing your eggs pretty, neat, and easy.

TISSUE PAPER is great for adding loose three-dimensional details like flower petals, and also for cushioning the eggs in gift boxes.

STICKERS also make instant designs possible and are great for kids.

Display finished eggs with panache!

We love collecting egg cups and other small vessels. Glass, china, and silver are all appealing. Whether you display your eggs in glassware, baskets, or take-out boxes, stay away from items with decorative patterns—you don't want to create competition. Your decorated eggs should take center stage!

Bejewels

Any pattern you can draw can be beaded on an egg.
Experiment—you might like the effect of matte beads instead of sparkly
glass ones, or want to begin with colored eggs.

gather

Lead pencil (#2)

Blown (see page 8) or hard-boiled
(see page 96) eggs, as many as desired,
clean and dry

Small flat paintbrush

Decoupage medium

Tiny marbles (beads without holes):
silver-green and periwinkle, or colors of
your choice (from the stamping section
of a crafts supply store)

create

1. Using the pencil, sketch a pattern for the beads on each egg; refer to
   the photo for ideas or devise a design of your own. If you wish to make
   a change, just erase the pencil line and redraw.
2. Paint decoupage medium onto one section of the sketched design and sprinkle beads onto the medium (press them lightly with the back of a spoon if
   they are not sticking). Wait a few minutes for the medium to dry.
3. Working on one section of the bead pattern at a time, repeat step 2
   until the pattern is complete. If your design has small motifs like the dots
   shown, you can cover a couple at a time.

tip If you are decorating several eggs, you can work on each in turn while the previous
one is drying. Pour the beads into small bowls or container lids so they're easy to pick
up—you can shake any that don't adhere to the egg back into the bowl before going on
to the next section of your design.

Chocolate Bunny's Backpack

Whether with dots, ducks, bows, or flowers, decorate the egg
with stickers chosen especially for the recipient of
this charming bunny.

gather

1 blown egg (see page 8), clean and dry

Small flat paintbrush

Lavender acrylic paint

Profile-style chocolate bunny,
7 inches tall

Cotton swab (optional)

Sparkle powder, from a cake decorating
supply vendor (optional)

Assorted small stickers (dots and
ducklings, as shown, or your choice)

Lavender ½-inch-wide twill tape or
ribbon, 16-inch piece

Small fresh or silk flower

create

1. Paint the egg (see page 9) and allow to dry.
2. Meanwhile, if you'd like to highlight the details on the bunny as we did,
   do so using a cotton swab dipped in the sparkle powder.
3. Affix stickers to the egg; use the photo as a guide or create your
   own design.
4. Rest the egg on the bunny's back and tie the twill tape around the
   bunny's neck so that it supports the egg (have a friend help by holding
   the egg while you tie). Make a neat knot or small bow and cut off the
   excess twill tape.
5. Embellish with a small flower.

tip Be sure to arrange the stickers thoughtfully on both sides of the egg so it looks
good when the bunny faces the other direction. You can use a dyed or plain egg instead
of the painted one if you wish.

Egg Gift Tag

This treasure of a tag makes clear your affection for
the one whose name it bears. The letters are purchased transfers,
so there's no need to worry about your handwriting.

gather

Transfer letters (in a size that will spell the desired name on the egg)

Small decorative motifs (from a crafts supply store)

1 blown egg (see page 8), clean and dry

Crafts Stick or pencil

³⁄₈-inch-wide ribbon, about 6 inches long

Glue gun and glue stick

create

1. Cut out the transfer letters and decorative motifs so you can apply them individually.
2. One at a time, apply each letter to the egg and, very gently, rub over them with a crafts stick or side of a pencil tip to transfer the design; then discard the acetate. Apply the decorative motifs around the name in the same way.
3. Insert one end of the ribbon into the hole in the top of the egg; secure with glue.
4. Tie the tag onto the ribbon of a wrapped gift.

tip If you'd like the gift tag to double as an ornament, use a longer piece of ribbon and insert both ends into the egg for a hanging loop; secure with glue.

Family Photo Memories

Remember special times with these charming photo-decorated eggs.
Start a tradition and give each loved one an egg every Easter.
For a different twist, use photos with a theme—flowers for your
garden club, teddy bears for your toddler's playgroup.

gather

Commercial egg dyes: assorted colors

Blown (see page 8) or hard-boiled
(see page 96) eggs, as many as desired,
clean and dry

Photocopies of family photos,
one for each egg

Decoupage medium

Small flat paintbrush

Wooden skewer

White acrylic paint

Small gift boxes (2 inches square),
decorative straw, and ribbon for giftwrap
(optional)

create

1. Prepare the dyes according to the package directions. Place each egg in
   a container of dye (see page 9); let sit for 20 minutes. Remove the eggs
   and place in an egg carton to dry.
2. Cut the copied photos to the size and shape you like. Adhere each to
   an egg using the decoupage medium and paintbrush. Let dry.
3. To add a decorative border, dip the end of the skewer (or the end of
   a small detail paintbrush handle) into paint and apply a pattern of
   dots around each photo (see page 9). Refer to the samples shown or
   create your own pattern. Let dry.
4. To package as gifts, nestle each egg in a box filled with decorative straw.
   Tie a ribbon around each box as shown.

tip To present the eggs as an album, pack a whole set in a larger box, or even in
an egg carton. Or for a fun display, use blown eggs and string them into a garland,
following the directions for the Wisp of Spring Garland on page 51.

Faux Filigree Eggs

Die-cut stickers from a crafts store are the secret to the delicate decoration of these eggs—the only talent you need is for arranging the designs. This technique gives equally lovely results on hard-boiled or blown eggs.

gather

Commercial egg dye: pink and lavender, or colors of your choice

Filigree stickers (from a crafts supply store)

Hard-boiled (see page 96) or blown (see page 8) eggs, as many as desired

create

1. Prepare the dyes according to the package directions.
2. Apply the stickers to the eggs. Refer to the photo for placement ideas or devise your own arrangements.
3. Place each egg in a container of dye (see page 9); let sit for 20 minutes. Remove the eggs and place in an egg carton to dry.
4. Peel off the stickers to reveal the filigree designs.

tip For multicolored eggs, dye the eggs lightly before you apply the stickers. and then dye them again, but in a different color, with the stickers in place.

Hydrangea Decoupage

Flower photocopies are the secret to these pretty eggs.
If hydrangeas are not in season, try any small blossoms that will
lie flat for copying—primroses, johnny-jump-ups, and tiny
daisies would be just as charming.

gather

1 fresh hydrangea flower cluster

Small flat paintbrushes,
½- and ¼-inch wide

Light blue acrylic paint

3 blown (see page 8) or hard-boiled (see
page 96) eggs (or as many as desired),
clean and dry

Decoupage medium

Basket, decorative straw,
foil-covered egg candies, decorated
egg-shape cookie, and a fresh or silk
hydrangea sprig for display

create

1. Cut the hydrangea blossoms apart. Make color photocopies of them
   and cut out the photocopied blossoms. You need 16 to 20 photocopied
   blossoms for each egg.
2. Using the larger paintbrush, paint the eggs light blue (see page 9) and set
   them aside to dry.
3. Referring to the photo and using the smaller paintbrush to apply the
   decoupage medium as glue, affix the cut-out blossoms on the eggs. Let dry.
4. Using the larger paintbrush, brush decoupage medium over the entire
   surface of each egg. Let dry.
5. To display the eggs, fill the basket with decorative straw. Arrange the
   candies, eggs, cookie, and hydrangea sprig on top.

tip The blossoms won't lie perfectly smoothly against the egg. Don't worry, that makes
them look more realistic, which is part of their appeal.

Lines of Poetry

Express your sentiments by wrapping an egg with favorite lines of poetry. Choose a beloved verse or write one to suit the occasion—you can even compose a love letter to make this egg the perfect gift for your sweetheart.

gather

Small flat paintbrush

Decoupage medium

Blown (see page 8) or hard-boiled (see page 96) eggs, as many as desired, clean and dry

create

1. Type your chosen poem so that you'll be able to cut the lines apart easily.
2. Print the poem and cut it into strips 3 to 5 inches long; be sure to cut between words, not through them.
3. One at a time, brush the back of the strips with decoupage medium and press each one onto an egg; overlap the strips slightly as you arrange them vertically, horizontally, or in any manner you like.
4. Repeat steps 2 and 3 for each egg, changing the color of the poem as you like. Let the eggs dry.

tip If you have a rotary cutter and cutting mat, use them to cut the poem apart quickly. Some inks run when coated with decoupage medium, so try to keep the front of the strips dry and don't put a top coat of medium over the finished egg.

Marbleized Eggs

These pretty swirled patterns are made by passing an egg through a bath of enamel paint suspended in water. The process is easy and the pleasantly unpredictable results are always a surprise.

gather

Enamel hobby paints: green, lavender, and purple, or colors of your choice

Disposable aluminum roasting pans, one for each color combination

Rubber gloves

Wooden skewers

Blown eggs (see page 8), as many as desired, clean and dry

Coffee filters

create

1. Decide the color or combinations you want to use—you may use one or more colors of paint for each marbling bath.
2. For each bath, fill a roasting pan with about 4 inches of water. Put on the rubber gloves. Add about 1 teaspoon of each color paint in the chosen combination. Swirl the end of a skewer through the paint.
3. Place an egg on the end of a skewer. Swirl it around through the paint and water. When the paint has adhered to the egg in a marbled pattern, remove the egg from the skewer to an egg carton and let it dry.
4. Repeat this process for each egg, using the different color marbleizing baths as you wish.
5. To dispose of paint responsibly, pour each bath slowly through a coffee filter, letting the water drain down the sink and capturing the paint. Throw away the paint.

tip If you wish, paint the eggs before marbleizing them; be sure to let them dry before dipping them in the marbleizing bath.

Pen and Ink Cartoons

Bring out your inner artist by drawing cute animals or portraits of loved ones on plain white blown eggs. Whether you copy a drawing from a book or magazine or do something unique, your characters are certain to charm.

gather

Lead pencil (# 2)	Small needle-nose pliers
Blown eggs (see page 8), as many as desired, clean and dry	Rayon tassel, 3½ inches long, for hair (one for each egg face)
Black permanent marker (extra-fine)	Glue gun and glue sticks or Tacky glue (optional)

create

1. Using the pencil, draw a design on each egg. If you wish to make a change, just gently erase the pencil line and redraw.
2. Make your designs permanent by drawing over them with the marker.
3. To add hair, use the pliers to gently enlarge the top hole and slip the knot end of the tassel into it. Let the tassel flop down; secure it with a little glue if necessary.

tip Enlarge the hole for the tassel before you draw the face—if the egg breaks, you won't have spoiled your drawing.

Ribbon and Candy-Flower Treats

Here's the perfect project to use up all those odds
and ends you can't bear to throw away or can't resist
buying at your favorite crafts store.

●

gather

Acrylic paint: pink or other desired colors	⅜-inch-wide ribbon, about 15 inches long for one egg
Small flat paintbrush	Glue gun and glue sticks or Tacky glue
Blown (see page 8) or hard-boiled (see page 96) eggs, as many as desired, clean and dry	Cake decorating flowers, 16 for one egg
	Wired pom-pom trim, 1½ yards for one egg

create

1. If you wish, paint the eggs (see page 9); let them dry.
2. For the ribbon egg, wrap the ribbon around the egg and cut it so that the ends meet. Glue the ribbon to the egg. To make the bow, cut and fold a 4-inch length of ribbon into a loop, overlap, and glue the ends. Then cut a 2-inch length of ribbon, flatten the loop, and cinch it with this short piece as shown in the photo on the facing page. Cut off any excess ribbon, glue the cinch closed, and then glue the bow to the ribbon on the egg.
3. For the candy-flower egg, glue the candies to the egg, arranging them in a random pattern.
4. For the pom-pom egg, cut the trim so there is a pom-pom right at the end. Glue this pom-pom to the top of the egg. Then wrap the trim vertically around the egg four times, spacing the wraps equally. Cut off the excess trim and glue the final pom-pom to the top of the egg. Adjust the spacing of the wrapped trim and affix it with more glue under a few pom-poms if needed.

tip These are so quick and easy to make and so festive, you might want to make them for a holiday bazaar. If so, buy the trimmings by the spool and, if you like, use foam eggs, as they are more durable.

Robin's-Egg Place Card

Guide your guests to their places at your Easter dinner table with these sweet springtime keepsakes. Add a few foil-covered chocolate eggs to the nest for an after-dinner or guest-room treat.

gather

Acrylic paint: light blue, brown, and white

Small flat paintbrush

Blown (see page 8) or hard-boiled (see page 96) eggs, one for each place card, clean and dry

Transfer letters (in a size that will spell the desired name on the egg)

Crafts stick or pencil

Small bird's nest, from a crafts supply store

Small natural-color feathers, 5 to 7 for each place card

create

1. Paint the egg blue (see page 9) and let it dry.
2. Spatter the egg, first with brown paint and then with white paint (see page 9), letting the paint dry between colors and before going on to the next step.
3. Cut out the transfer letters so you can apply them individually.
4. One at a time and working very gently, apply each letter to the egg, rub over the acetate with a crafts stick or side of a pencil tip to transfer the design, and then discard the acetate.
5. Place the egg in the nest and tuck a few feathers around it.

tip If you are making a set of place cards, work in assembly-line style, doing one step on all the eggs before going on to the next step. Make some extra spatter-painted eggs in case one breaks when you are rubbing the letters into place. If your handwriting is neat, you might like to write each name with a brown marker instead of using transfer letters.

Scrapbook Charm Eggs

To find trimmings for these fun eggs, visit the scrapbook section at the crafts store—there are so many options, you'll want to do this project by the dozen. Why not add hanging loops and turn them into great ornaments?

gather

Acrylic paint: assorted seasonal colors

Small flat paintbrush

Blown (see page 8) or hard-boiled (see page 96) eggs, clean and dry

Glue gun and glue sticks or Tacky glue

Scrapbook embellishments, assorted sizes and styles

create

1. Paint each egg one color (see page 9) and let it dry.
2. Glue embellishments onto each egg in a striped or random pattern or even cover the egg completely; refer to the photo for ideas or devise patterns of your choice.
3. Let the glue dry.

tip For a pretty array, leave some eggs white and choose white embellishments for the colored eggs. Tweezers are handy for positioning these small decorations.

Seedling Sprouter

Herbs, flowers, and even vegetables will get a good start in this little eggshell planter. For a gift or a children's project, arrange a small garden of these in an egg carton.

gather

Small needle-nose pliers

Blown eggs (see page 8), one for each seedling, clean and dry

Acrylic paint: chartreuse and yellow

Small flat paintbrush

Potting soil

Spoon

1 or 2 seeds for each egg

Salt well, egg cup, or other small dish

create

1. Using the pliers and your fingertips, gently chip away the top third of the eggshell to form a cup as shown in the photo.
2. Paint the outside of the egg chartreuse, then paint the inside yellow (see page 9); let dry.
3. Spoon a little potting soil into the shell, leaving the top quarter empty.
4. Plant one or two seeds, covering with soil according to the seed packet directions.
5. Set the egg planter in the salt well. Add water to moisten the soil. Place on your windowsill and wait for the seedling to appear.

tip If the sprouter doesn't sit upright in your dish, put some sand in the dish first to support the egg. When it's time to plant the seedling in your garden, plant it right in the eggshell. Compost!

Silver and Gold

Perfectly precious, these gold- and silver-leafed eggs are
lovely when displayed in a bowl and delightful as party favors or
prizes for an egg hunt.

●

Small flat paintbrushes

Blown eggs (see page 8), as many as
desired, clean and dry

Decoupage medium

Synthetic gold or silver leaf,
3 sheets for each egg (from an art
or crafts supply store)

create

1. Using a paintbrush, cover an egg entirely with decoupage medium.
2. Immediately place a sheet of gold or silver leaf on the egg, pressing lightly
   onto the surface with the brush handle. Place two more sheets of leaf on
   the egg, pressing each onto the egg and covering it completely.
3. To enhance the sheen, brush repeatedly over the leaf-covered egg with the
   bristle end of a clean, dry paintbrush. Set the egg aside and let it dry.
4. Repeat this process for each egg.

tip Metal leaf is very lightweight and tends to blow around while you work with it.
To minimize mess, position your work area away from open windows and out of the path
of any fans.

Spring Pansy Vase

So simple, so sweet. Make one of these for someone special (could be you) or make enough to place one by every setting at your table. Fill the vase with lilies of the valley, forget-me-nots, or rosebuds as the season passes.

gather

Small needle-nose pliers

1 blown egg (see page 8), clean and dry

Epoxy glue

Salt well or other small dish, for the base

Small, single-stem flowers, such as pansies or violas

Card stock for tag (optional)

create

1. Using the pliers, gently chip away the shell around the hole in the top of the egg, enlarging it to the size of a pea.

2. To make the vase watertight, put a small dot of epoxy glue over the hole in the bottom of the egg. Let it dry.

3. Fill the vase with water. Set it on the base.

4. Arrange a few small flowers in the vase.

5. Create a paper tag with a seasonal thought or the name of a guest or recipient of a gift, if desired.

tip We chose a salt well to support the vase. You can use an egg cup, a small vase, or even a demitasse cup. Fill the container with salt or sand to steady the vase if it doesn't stand upright.

Strawbunnies

Make a big family of these bunnies for party
favors for a picnic or a children's party.

gather

Tracing paper	Glue gun and glue stick
Lead pencil (#2)	One 2-by-12-inch scrap of fabric for the collar and tie
Scraps of card stock: white, pink, blue, and yellow	
	Hand-sewing needle and thread
2 blown eggs (see page 8), or number desired, sterilized and dry	White masking tape
	Drinking straws, one for each egg
Ultra-fine-tip black permanent marker	

create

1. Trace the patterns for the ears, nose, and hat on page 93 onto tracing paper; cut them out. For each pair of ears, cut two pieces of white card stock and two of pink card stock. Use pink card stock for each nose. For each set of whiskers, cut a $^3/_4$-by-1$^1/_2$-inch piece of pink into six strips.
2. Using the pencil, sketch a face on each egg. Go over the sketched lines with the marker. Glue a nose and whiskers to the face. Center and glue each pink ear on a white one, then glue each pair of ears to an egg; make one set point down so the ears are floppy.
3. Use the patterns to cut out the hat side, brim, and top from blue card stock. Roll the side piece into a cylinder, overlap the ends, and glue to secure the shape. Fold up the notches around the hat top and put a little glue around the inside edge of the cylinder. Insert the top, notches-down, into the cylinder. Put some glue on the notched sections of the brim; center the brim, glue-side up, under the cylinder and press the notches up against the inside. Cut and glue a skinny yellow band around the hat as shown in the photo. Glue the hat to the egg with the floppy ears.
4. For a bowtie, cut a strip of fabric $^1/_2$ by 6 inches. Tie it around a straw. For a collar, cut a strip of fabric 1$^1/_2$ by 12 inches. With the needle and thread, gather one long edge, wrap the collar around a straw, and tie the threads to secure the gathers.
5. Cover the top hole of the upright-eared egg with a snippet of tape. Slide each egg onto the appropriate straw.

Tiny Chalkboards

Look no further for the perfect egg decorating party
activity—kids of all ages will have a blast
with this. Have the eggs painted black ahead of time
so everyone can delve right in and draw.

gather

Blown eggs (see page 8), as many as
desired, clean and dry

Black chalkboard paint (spray or brush-on)

Small flat paintbrush (if using
brush-on paint)

Colored chalk

Paper towel

Tiny magnets and glue (optional)

create

1. Paint the eggs (see page 9) and let them dry. If you are using spray paint, work outdoors or in a ventilated space.
2. To create a bond for the designs, cover the surface of each egg with any color chalk and then, using a paper towel, gently rub off the chalk.
3. Draw a design on each egg freehand, using as many colors as you like.
4. If you'd like to display an egg on your refrigerator or a memo board, glue a tiny magnet to its back.

tip Young kids will love doing this project. Remind them to be gentle with their chalk drawings—eggshells are not made of slate! You can also use hard-boiled eggs for this project, but if you do, don't eat them.

Easter Dinner Menu

pineapple glazed ham
herbed mashed potatoes
candied carrots
sauteed string beans
lemon meringue pie
bunny cookies

Tulip Menu Card

Anticipation will be high when you announce your holiday
feast with these festive menu cards. For a buffet,
adapt this idea to create a name card for each dish.

gather

Tracing paper

Yellow card stock (one 8½-by-11-inch
piece for each menu and stand)

White glue or rubber cement

Dremel drill and mandrel bit fitted
with a cut-off wheel

Blown eggs (see page 8), clean and dry,
one for each holder

Floral stickers, ¼- and ½-inch
diameter (or use any motif you like)

create

1. Trace the tulip pattern on page 94 onto tracing paper and cut it out.
2. Using a computer (or hand-lettering), compose and print your menu on
   card stock, positioning the text so the tulip pattern can be centered over
   it. Center the pattern over the menu and trace the tulip outline. Cut it
   out. Repeat to make as many menus as you need.
3. For each egg stand, cut a piece of card stock measuring ½ by 4 inches.
   Form it into a ring, overlapping the ends slightly, and glue together.
4. Using the drill and referring to the photo on page 7, gently cut a slot in
   the top of each egg to hold the menu card.
5. Affix stickers to each egg and stand. Set the eggs into the stands and
   insert a menu card in each. Put one at each diner's place when you set your
   holiday table.

tip Use paper clips or doll-size clothespins to secure the holder rings while the glue dries.

Watercolor Vines in Grass

Greening grass is a welcome sign of spring, and it is a traditional hiding spot for Easter eggs. These tendril-painted eggs come with their own little plots of grass—see how many friends can spot them if you hide them outdoors.

gather

Small liner paintbrush

Watercolor paints: light and medium green

1 blown (see page 8) or hard-boiled (see page 96) egg (or as many as desired), clean and dry

Small pot of grass (from a pet store), for display

create

1. Dip the paintbrush in light green paint. Starting at the bottom of the egg, make a long, curving, vine-like stroke up toward the top. Repeat to paint one or two more curving vines.
2. Paint small leaves at intervals along both sides of each vine; leave a bit of white space between the leaves and their vine. Let the paint dry.
3. Using the darker green paint, add a thin stem from the vine into the center of each leaf. Let the paint dry.
4. Nest the egg in the pot of grass.

tip If you are painting a lot of these vine eggs, paint the light green vines and leaves on all the eggs, then paint all the dark green stems. Paint a single vine in a spiral around some of the eggs. Or paint some of the eggs solid green first, then paint with white vines.

Wisp of Spring Garland

The garland shown on the facing page is about five feet long; you can make yours any length and vary the number and spacing of the eggs. Decorate a table or mantel with one, hang several in the window, or drape them on an Easter tree.

gather

Fine-tip permanent markers, in several seasonal colors

7 blown eggs (see page 8), clean and dry

2 yards ⅝-inch-wide sheer ribbon

Masking or transparent tape

Small wooden skewer (pointed on both ends)

create

1. Using the markers, decorate the eggs—stripes and dots look great, but use spirals, squiggles, or other simple design, too, as you wish.
2. Tie the ribbon in a knot near one end. Tape the other end to the skewer.
3. Thread the skewer through an egg. Gently slide the egg against the knot. Tie a knot in the ribbon at the other end of the egg.
4. Knot the ribbon again, about 8 inches away from the egg. Thread the skewer through another egg. Knot the ribbon again at the other end of this egg. Continue in this manner until all the eggs are on the ribbon.

tip An upholsterer's needle or a bodkin—a long metal tool with a little clamp on one end, designed for threading cord through small channels—would be a great substitute for the skewer and tape. You'll find both at a good crafts supply store.

Yarn Wraparounds

Yarns are so beautiful, you'll want to make dozens of these eggs using a rainbow of colors and textures. Try combining yarns to make stripes or cover each half of an egg in a different color.

gather

Glue gun and glue sticks

Yarn, 6 to 8 yards per egg

Blown (see page 8) or hard-boiled (see page 96) eggs, as many as desired, clean and dry

Decorative bowl, jelly beans, small leafy branch, white chocolate bunny, and ball of yarn for display (optional)

create
1. Glue one end of the yarn to one end of an egg.
2. Wrap the yarn in a spiral around the egg; cover the surface completely, securing the yarn with small dots of glue as you go.
3. Secure the yarn at the other end of the egg and cut off any excess.
4. Repeat this process to cover each egg.
5. If you wish to make a centerpiece as shown, fill the bowl with jelly beans, form the branch into a hoop and tuck it into the bowl, add the bunny and a ball of yarn, and top the yarn with a wrapped egg.

tip You can also wrap the yarn vertically over the ends of the egg, using a circular motion rather than a spiral. It's hard to believe you need so much yarn to wrap a single egg, but you'll see how much you use as you go!

Candles on the Half Shell

Be sure to use extra-large eggs for this project so you'll be able to fit a candle into each. Arrange the candles in a group or place one at each diner's place on your dinner table.

gather

Small flat paintbrush

Rose-pink acrylic paint

Blown eggs (see page 8), clean and dry, one for each holder

Small needle-nose pliers

Tea lights, one for each candle

Eggcups, one for each candle

create

1. Paint the eggs (see page 9) and let them dry.
2. Using the pliers and your fingertips, gently chip away the top third of each eggshell.
3. Insert a tea light into each eggshell and set the eggshell into an eggcup.

tip If the tea lights don't sit level in the eggshells, gently tip them out. Put a small piece of crushed wax paper into each shell, then reinsert the tea lights.

Countdown to Easter!

Consume one glass of sweets each day in anticipation of Sunday.

7 blown eggs (see page 8), clean and dry

Acrylic paint: white, rose, and lavender shades

Small paintbrushes

Small needle-nose pliers

Card stock: white and scrap of a contrast color

Tacky glue or tape

Wooden skewers

7 assorted clear glasses: juice, cordial, sherbet, and eggcup sizes

Assorted small Easter candies: jelly beans, foil-wrapped chocolates

Orange yarn, 10-inch piece

Profile-style chocolate bunny, 7 inches tall

create

1. Paint the eggs assorted lavender and rose colors; let them dry. Then, referring to the photo on the facing page, add dot designs to five eggs. Using the pliers and your fingertips, gently chip away the shells on the two remaining eggs to form cups as shown.
2. Type the day names "Monday" through "Saturday" and "Easter," and print them on the card stock. If you like, create no-color letters and fill the background with color. (Or, if you prefer, hand-letter them.)
3. Cut out the tags in banner shapes; glue some of them onto larger pieces of card stock and cut out again to create borders. Glue or tape some of the banners to wooden skewers.
4. Fill the glasses with assorted candies. Arrange the glasses in a line. Top each with an egg and banner, gluing the banners in place if necessary.
5. Tie the yarn around the bunny's neck and then to the stem of the "Easter" glass. Scatter more candies around your display.

tip Use small stencils to make some of the dot designs (see page 9 for stenciling directions). To make a slot in the top of an egg for one of the banners, use a Dremel drill with a mandrel bit fitted with a cut-off wheel, as shown on page 7.

Cupboard Tassel

Decorative tassels make wayward keys easy to spot, and
they look pretty hanging on a cupboard, armoire, or trunk
when the key is inserted in the lock.

gather

Small needle-nose pliers

1 blown egg (see page 8), clean and dry

1 off-white tassel, 5 inches long

Acrylic paint: sky blue, brown, and white

Small paintbrushes: flat, small stencil,
and fine-tipped detail

Mini-scallop stencil in Mylar
(from a crafts supply store)

Glue gun and glue stick

Small key

Hemp string, 6-inch-long piece

create

1. Using the pliers, gently chip away the shell around the bottom hole in the egg, enlarging it enough to slide over the tassel top. Enlarge the top hole slightly so the tassel cord loop will fit through it easily. (Remove the tassel before doing the next step.)
2. Paint the egg sky blue (see page 9) and let it dry.
3. Referring to the photo on the facing page, paint the decorative pattern on the egg: Use the scallop stencil (see page 9 for stenciling directions) for the white pattern around the middle and add a brown highlight to it free-hand with the fine-tipped brush. Paint the other designs freehand, using the end of the brush handle to make the dots (see page 9). Let dry.
4. Insert the tassel top in the egg, passing the cord loop out through the top hole. Secure the tassel to the bottom hole with a small amount of glue, if necessary.
5. Attach the key with the hemp string as pictured.

tip If the tassel cord loop doesn't slide through the top hole easily, use a crochet hook to pull it through.

Easter Wreath

Elegant in its simplicity, this wreath looks great hanging or lying flat on a table as part of an Easter vignette. If your wreath form doesn't have a hanging wire, attach one before you decorate it.

gather

6 to 7 dozen blown eggs (see page 8), clean and dry

Acrylic paint: assorted shades of lavender and blue

Small flat paintbrush

11-inch-diameter green Styrofoam wreath form

Glue gun and glue sticks

1 package sheet moss (410 cubic inches)

create

1. Paint the eggs assorted shades (see page 9) and let dry.
2. Place the wreath form on a work surface. Referring to the photo on the facing page, glue the eggs, one at a time and top-end in, around the inside of the wreath.
3. Glue another ring of eggs to the top of the wreath, placing them close to the inside. To keep the effect informal, vary the angle at which you affix them and turn some of them top-end up.
4. Glue a third ring of eggs closer to the outside of the wreath top, then glue one last ring of eggs around the outside of the wreath.
5. Tear the sheet moss into small pieces. One small area at a time, put some glue in the crevices between the eggs and press some moss into the glue. Cover all exposed portions of the wreath form with the moss.

tip For a different spin on this wreath, use brilliantly colored eggs or even patterned ones, and replace the moss with excelsior (Easter-basket grass) or decorative straw.

Feathered Eggs-on-a-Twig

"Whimsical" only begins to describe these little heralds of
the spring. They'll have a slightly different demeanor
depending on which end of the egg you choose for the beak,
so experiment with that—and try different-size eggs, too.

gather

Blown eggs (see page 8), one for each bird, clean and dry

Acrylic paint: light blue and yellow or colors of your choice

Small paintbrush

Scrap of yellow card stock for beaks

Glue gun and glue sticks

Seed beads for eyes

Small fluffy feathers: colors to match or contrast the paint

Tapestry needle, size 16

Terry-cloth towel (to pad your worktable)

Small hammer

Small twigs for legs (about 1 inch long each)

create

1. Paint each egg one color (see page 9) and let it dry.
2. For each beak, fold the card stock in half and then cut a long triangle (about half an inch high) through both layers, placing the base along the fold.
3. Glue the folded end of a beak over the hole at one end of each egg.
4. Referring to the photo on the facing page, glue seed beads to the eggs for the birds' eyes.
5. Glue the feathers in place on one egg at time, attaching two large feathers in the remaining hole for a tail, two feathers on each side for wings, and one small feather under the beak. (Cut a fragment for this if your feathers are too big.)
6. For the legs, use the tapestry needle to pierce two holes in the bottom of each egg: Place the egg on a folded towel, and tap the eye end of the needle gently with the hammer. Insert a twig in each hole, gluing to secure.

tip If you'd like to hang the birds as ornaments, cut a length of fishing line for the hanger and glue one end to each side, under the wing feathers when you attach them.

Good Night-Light

Banish fear of the dark with this charming
night-light cover. It's fragile, so be sure you turn it
on and off for your small child.

gather

Needle-nose pliers

1 blown goose egg (see page 8),
clean and dry

Night-light base and bulb

White ½-inch-wide masking tape

Tracing paper

Black card stock or colored paper,
3 inches square

Craft knife

Small flat paintbrush

Decoupage medium

Pencil or wooden skewer

Scrap of ½-inch-wide ribbon

Tacky glue

create

1. Using the pliers, gently chip away the shell at the bottom of the egg,
   enlarging the hole so it fits over the lightbulb and sits on the night-
   light base.
2. Reinforce the opening by folding a piece of masking tape over the edge.
3. Trace a bunny pattern (see page 95) onto tracing paper and cut it out. Use
   it to cut one bunny from the card stock, using the craft knife to cut the
   tail detail.
4. Brush decoupage medium over one side of the bunny cutout. Insert the
   cutout in the egg, pressing the coated side against the side of the egg
   (use the pencil or skewer to hold the bunny in place until it begins to
   adhere). Let the cutout dry.
5. Wrap the ribbon around the base of the night-light as shown in the photo
   on the facing page; secure with Tacky glue.

tip Carefully bend the cutout in half vertically so you can easily insert it into the egg,
but make sure not to crease it. It doesn't matter if it adheres a bit crookedly; that will
just add to its charm. To purchase a goose egg, see the Resources section on page 95.

Posy Party Lights

Welcome the Easter Bunny and your guests by hanging lots of strings of these sparkling lights in your windows or draping them on a buffet. Make the flowers multicolored if you like, or make each string a different color—go for round, pointed, or serrated petals, too.

gather

Dremel drill and mandrel bit fitted with a cut-off wheel

Blown eggs (see page 8), one for each bulb on the light string, clean and dry

Small needle-nose pliers

Card stock: shades of pink or colors of your choice

Glue gun and glue stick or Tacky glue

String of mini-lights

White electrical tape

create

1. Referring to the photo on page 7 and using the drill, cut off the top quarter of the eggshell; discard the top.
2. Using the pliers, gently chip away the shell around the hole in each egg, enlarging it sufficiently to fit over a lightbulb.
3. Using the patterns on page 92, cut one, two, or more petal shapes from the card stock. Cut 12 identical petals for each egg (depending on which pattern you choose and the size of your egg, you may need a few more or a few less).
4. Glue the petals to the outside of each egg as shown in the photo on the facing page; lightly fold back each petal before attaching it.
5. Fit each egg posy over a lightbulb; secure the outside of the shell to the light cord with white tape.

tip You might like to draw designs on the petals or eggs with a marker. If you decide to do this, do it before attaching the petals to the egg shell.

Secondhand Rose Egg

Collectors of vintage fashions and textiles will love this pretty egg with its scrap-basket trimmings. Decorate it with old or new millinery flowers (the kind with wired petals, stems, or leaves) so you can tweak them into the perfect position.

gather

Small flat paintbrush

Pink acrylic paint
(or a color that goes with your fabric)

1 blown egg (see page 8),
clean and dry

Scrap of vintage-style fabric,
at least 2 by 12 inches

Small cloth and bead millinery flowers

Tacky glue

Decorative metal basket or other
container to hold egg

create

1. Paint the egg (see page 9) and let it dry.
2. Snip the edge of the fabric and tear it into a strip about 1 by 10 inches. (Some fabrics won't tear; if this is the case, cut the strip instead.)
3. Wrap the fabric strip around the egg as shown in the photo on the facing page and tie in a knot or small bow.
4. Tuck the cloth flower under the knot; adjust the blossom, leaves, and stem as you like. Add the bead flower. Secure these embellishments with glue if necessary.
5. Place the egg in your container.

tip For a container, look in flea markets for vintage plant holders, soap dishes, wire baskets, or similar garden or kitchen accessories. Look there for millinery flowers, too, or at a fabric store.

Springtime Mobile

How clever! A lampshade forms the support for this diminutive mobile, so it's easy to balance these pretty batiked eggs.

gather

10 blown eggs (see page 8), clean and dry

White crayon

Commercial egg dyes: orange and green

Small white lampshade, 9 inches in diameter at the lower edge

Tapestry needle, size 16

White glue

¼-inch-wide ribbons: ½ yard each orange polka dot and light green

20 transparent plastic hole reinforcements

Glue gun and glue sticks or Tacky glue (optional)

5 yards hemp string, cut into 10 pieces, each 18 inches long

create

1. To make the batik patterns on the eggs, use the white crayon to draw a design on each egg. Prepare the dyes according to the package directions. Submerge half the eggs in the orange dye and half in the green dye; let sit for 20 minutes. Remove the eggs and place in an egg carton to dry.
2. Meanwhile, prepare the shade. Using the tapestry needle, poke 10 holes, evenly spaced and about ¼ inch above the bottom edge of the shade. Glue the ribbons around the shade above the holes as shown in the photo on the facing page. Hang shade so you'll be able to arrange the eggs on it.
3. When the eggs are dry, affix a paper reinforcement over each hole (add a dab of glue if they don't adhere completely).
4. Tie a knot in one end of each piece of string. Thread the tapestry needle with a length of string and, inserting from bottom to top, pass it all the way through one of the eggs (make sure the knot is large enough to support the egg), then pass the needle through one of the holes in the shade. Tie the twine to itself as pictured, setting the top of the egg about 3 inches below the shade.
5. Repeat step 4 with the remaining eggs, alternating colors and allowing about ¾ inch more string between the shade and each subsequent egg. Adjust the twine length if needed and cut off the excess.

Sunday Centerpiece

As simple and fresh as the first spring breeze, this arrangement is as perfect for your breakfast or brunch table as it is for an Easter dinner buffet. Use silk flowers instead of fresh if you'd like the centerpiece to last more than a day or two.

gather

Small paintbrush	Flower frog or florist foam
Acrylic paint: pale yellow and light green	Glass compote or pretty bowl
6 blown eggs (see page 8), or number needed for your container, clean and dry	Assorted fresh flowers, such as lavender, daisies, pansies, coreopsis, or tulips

create

1. Paint the eggs (see page 9) and let them dry.
2. Place the flower frog in the compote. Add about 2 inches of water.
3. Arrange the eggs in the compote. Insert the flowers one stem at a time, making sure each stem end is in the water and fitting them into the frog or foam to control their angle.
4. Place the compote in the center of your table.

tip To figure out how many eggs you need, do a test arrangement before you begin. When you do the final arrangement, rotate the compote to check the composition from all sides.

Sweet Stenciled Eggs

A tisket, a tasket—this tiny stenciled basket and its whimsical companion eggs will bring a smile to every face.

gather

Dremel drill and mandrel bit fitted with a cut-off wheel

Blown eggs (see page 8), as many as desired, clean and dry

Acylic paint: yellow and assorted colors

Paintbrushes: flat, stencil, and detail

Small stencils: basket weave, star, and spiral (or designs of your choice)

3 small, flexible twigs, each about 5 inches long (for the basket handle)

Masking tape

Glue gun and glue sticks

Glass compote, jelly beans, and shredded colored paper for display (optional)

create

1. To make the basket, use the drill to cut off the top half of an egg (refer to the photo on page 7).
2. Paint the eggs yellow (see page 9) and let dry.
3. Plan the arrangement of the stencil designs; refer to the photo on the facing page for ideas or devise your own designs. Lightly pencil on your design. Stencil the eggs (see page 9); complete all of one color and let dry before changing to another color. Use the end of a round paintbrush handle to add small painted dots (see page 9).
4. To complete the basket egg, twist the small twigs together gently and bend them into a U; wrap together at each end with tape. Glue them to the inside of the egg for a handle (hold one end until set, then glue the other end and hold until set). Highlight the handle with diluted yellow paint if you wish.
5. For a centerpiece, fill the compote with jelly beans. Fill the basket egg with shredded colored paper and jelly beans; gently nestle it into the compote so it sits upright.

tip For darling ornaments, make a bunch of basket eggs, fill them with something very lightweight (like decorative straw and feather chicks or silk blossoms), and hang them from your Easter tree.

Tic Tac Toe

In case you've forgotten, Tic Tac Toe is played on a grid
of nine squares by two players, each of whom tries, in alternating
turns, to place his mark—either X or O—in three
consecutive squares. We used an egg-serving dish as our playing
board, but you can easily make one from an egg carton.

gather

Fruit leather, color and flavor
of your choice

Acrylic cutting board or waxed paper

1-inch cookie cutters in the shapes
of the letters O and X

10 hard-boiled eggs (see page 96)

Toothpick or small skewer

Egg carton

Clear tape

create

1. Unroll the fruit leather on the cutting board. Using the cookie cuttters,
   cut out five of each letter.
2. Place each cut-out letter on an egg, close to the narrower end. The
   letters will adhere on their own; use the toothpick to ease them into
   position if needed.
3. Cut the egg carton, piecing it to form a square with three cups on
   each edge; tape the pieces together.
4. Give one player all the X eggs and the other player all the O eggs.
   You're set to play—Tic Tac Toe!

tip A liner from a fruit shipping crate will also make a good game board.
So would an ornament storage box. Or how about your collection of egg cups?

Topiary Sur la Table

You'll need a lot of blown eggs to make this sculptural egg tree, but it's one you'll be able to keep for years to come.

gather

7 dozen blown eggs (see page 8), clean and dry

Green Styrofoam cone topiary form, 15 inches tall

Glue gun and glue sticks

Yellow latex spray paint

1 bag Spanish moss (125 cubic inches/2 liters)

1 pound Jordan almonds in assorted colors

Footed bowl or other container

Bubble wrap and sturdy box, for storage (optional)

create

1. Beginning at the bottom and referring to the photo on the facing page, glue the eggs, one at a time and top-end in, in a ring around the form.
2. Glue a second ring of eggs just above the first; vary the angle of the eggs and attach some with the bottom end against the form, as seems natural and interesting.
3. Continue to glue the eggs in rings until you reach the top of the form. Glue a single egg, bottom-end down, to the top.
4. Working in a ventilated place on a protected surface, spray the topiary with spray paint. Let it dry. Spray again if necessary for full coverage. Let dry.
5. Tear the Spanish moss into small wisps. One at a time, put a dab of glue in each crevice between the eggs and tuck a wisp of moss into it. Glue Jordan almonds into most of the crevices.
6. To store the topiary from one Easter to the next, remove it from the bowl or container, pack it carefully in bubble wrap in a box and put it in a cool, dry place.

tip Our topiary sits on top of the container rim, supported by the eggs. If you want to make sure your topiary is secure in the container you choose, cut a piece of foam to fit the container, insert a small dowel in the center of the topiary bottom, and push the dowel down into the foam in the container.

Chocolate-Filled Delights

Imagine the surprise of friends who open these
hard-boiled look-alikes to find them filled with chocolate.
Give yourself time to make these; they need sufficient
drying and hardening before they can be enjoyed.

gather

Blown eggs (see page 8), as many as
desired, sterilized and dry,
with egg cartons to hold them all

Flat ½-inch-wide paintbrush

Brown food coloring (mix red and green if
you don't have brown)

Masking tape

Small needle-nose pliers

Baking chips, white, milk, and dark
chocolate flavors, 1 cup per egg

Plastic food storage bags, 1 gallon size

create

1. Spatter each egg (see page 9) with food coloring. Allow them to dry for
   several hours.
2. Seal the hole in the wider end of each blown egg with a small piece of
   masking tape. Using the pliers, gently chip away the shell around the other
   hole, enlarging it to the size of a pea. Place the eggs in an egg carton,
   open-end up.
3. One at a time, fill the eggs with chocolate: Place 1 cup of the baking chips
   in a food storage bag and twist the bag like a pastry bag to secure the
   chips in one bottom corner. Microwave on medium for 1 minute, until soft.
   Snip the corner from the bag and pipe the chocolate into the egg, tapping
   the egg periodically to compress any air bubbles and filling it completely,
   to the top of the hole.
4. Refrigerate the eggs overnight so the chocolate is firm. Remove the
   masking tape. Store in the refrigerator if not eating soon.
5. Tap the eggs on the table to crack the shells, and peel. Yum.

tip Be patient! Don't try to melt more than 1 cup of chocolate at a time—the
chocolate consistency may change and it will cool too quickly to fill multiple eggs.

Crackled Mosaic Eggs

Broken eggshells are a must for this technique; you can dye and then break some eggs or recycle accidentally crushed pieces from other projects. Use dyed eggs as a base and white fragments if you like.

gather

Commercial egg dyes: yellow, purple, and orange, or colors of your choice

Blown eggs (see page 8), one or more for each color dye and one for each egg to be decorated, clean and dry

Lead pencil (#2)

Decoupage medium

Small flat paintbrush

create

1. Decide how many colors you want in your mosaic. Prepare the dye for each according to the package directions.
2. Dye one egg each color (see page 9). If you are making a lot of mosaic eggs, dye more than one egg each color. Let the eggs dry.
3. Gently break the dyed eggs into small pieces. Keep the colors separate.
4. Using the pencil, sketch a pattern for the mosaic on an egg; refer to the photo on the facing page for an idea or devise a design of your own.
5. Paint decoupage medium onto one section of the sketched design and press the dyed eggshell pieces, one at a time, onto the medium; fill the entire section. Wait a few minutes for the medium to dry.
6. Working on one section of the mosaic pattern at a time, repeat step 5 until the pattern is complete. Let the egg dry.
7. Brush decoupage medium over the entire surface of the egg. Let dry.

Fanciful Flowering Stems

Call them peonies, camellias, exotic tulips, or made-up posies—
here are the makings of a spring bouquet that will never fade.

gather

Acrylic paint: assorted seasonal colors

Small paintbrush

Blown eggs (see page 8), one for each flower, clean and dry

Tissue paper, assorted seasonal colors, including yellow and green

Small pair of scissors with a pointed tip

Glue gun and glue sticks

Lollipop sticks, one for each egg

Lightweight floral wire

Wire cutter

Clear glass or small vase and small colorful candies for display (optional)

create

1. Paint the eggs (see page 9) and let them dry.
2. Using a photocopier, enlarge the petal patterns on page 92 to be about 8 inches long (400%). Cut out each pattern.
3. Cut the colored tissue paper into 9-inch squares, ten squares for each flower. Stack the layers for each flower you wish to make.
4. Place a pattern on a tissue paper stack and draw around it and cut out the shape through all ten layers. Repeat for each flower.
5. Using the tip of a small sharp pair of scissors, poke a small hole in the center of each cut-out stack of tissue paper.
6. Cut yellow and green tissue paper into 1½-by-6-inch strips. Starting at one corner, roll up each strip diagonally, then twist tightly. Referring to the photo on the facing page, insert a few "stamens" in the top of each egg and glue in place.
7. Place a small amount of glue around one end of a lollipop stick and insert it into the bottom of an egg; hold until set. Repeat for remaining eggs.
8. Thread a stack of petals onto each lollipop stick. Rotate and fan the layers and lift them up around the egg. Secure by wrapping with wire.
9. To display the flowers, put some small colorful candies in the bottom of the glass, then insert the lollipop "stems."

Goldfish Cupcake Toppers

You'll giggle with each eye you attach to these fish, and so will everyone to whom you serve one. If your taste runs to tropical fish, by all means, go for other colors.

gather

Small foam paintbrush

Orange acrylic paint or food-safe dye

Blown eggs (see page 8), clean and dry, one for each goldfish

Tracing paper, for patterns

Orange card stock or construction paper

Tacky glue

Orange tissue paper

Small googly eyes, 2 for each goldfish

Frosted cupcakes

create

1. Paint the eggs (see page 9) and let them dry.
2. Trace the patterns on page 94 onto tracing paper and cut them out. Use them for the following steps.
3. Cut out one mouth from the card stock or construction paper. Fold it in half; then curve the open ends away from each other as shown. Insert the folded end into one of the holes in an egg. Secure with a drop of glue if necessary.
4. Using the patterns, cut one top fin, two side fins, and two tail fins from tissue paper. Fold each piece back at the dotted line. Place glue on the small folded section and place on an egg as pictured.
5. Glue a googly eye on each side of the face.
6. Place a goldfish on top of a frosted cupcake.
7. Repeat steps 3 through 6 as many times as needed for the number of toppers you are making.

Good Fortune Eggs

These eggs sparkle so prettily, no one will want to break them open . . . until you let them know that inside are tiny edible treats—and a fortune that will come true!

gather

Small needle-nose pliers	Sheet of plain paper
Blown eggs (see page 8), sterilized and dry	Masking or transparent tape
Tissue paper, one colored sheet for each egg, plus a scrap of white	Dragees or sprinkles, about 2 tablespoons for each egg
Small foam paintbrush	Printed fortunes, one for each egg
Decoupage medium	Superfine glitter, one or more colors
	Clean cardboard ½-pint takeout food containers, one for each egg

create

1. Using the pliers, gently chip away the shell around one hole in each blown egg, enlarging it to the size of a pea.
2. Tear the scrap of white tissue paper into pieces just large enough to cover the holes in the eggs.
3. Using the paintbrush and decoupage medium, affix a piece of torn tissue paper over the smaller hole in each egg; set aside to dry.
4. Roll the piece of paper into a cone and snip a small piece off the end; make sure the open end will fit into the open hole in the egg and tape the paper to secure the shape.
5. Pour some dragees or sprinkles into each egg through the paper cone; don't fill the egg completely. Roll up a fortune and insert it into the egg.
6. Affix a piece of white tissue paper over the second hole and let it dry.
7. One at a time, brush the eggs with decoupage medium, sprinkle with glitter until covered, and set aside to dry.
8. Place a sheet of colored tissue paper into each takeout food container (crush the center of the paper to pad the bottom of the container). Nestle an egg into the tissue and close the container.

...s say lucky egg brings new life

Lovely Lacy Egg

A window is the perfect place to hang this delicate egg, which will look so pretty with light filtering through the holes. Keep your design simple so the perforated outline can be easily seen.

gather

Small needle-nose pliers	Small hammer
1 blown egg (see page 8), clean and dry	¼-inch-wide ribbon, ½ yard
Lead pencil (#2)	Glue gun and glue stick
Terry-cloth towel (to pad your worktable)	½-inch-wide ribbon, ½ yard
Tapestry needles, large and small	Small vintage-style pin or button

create

1. Using the pliers, gently chip away the shell around the hole in the top of the egg, enlarging it to the size of a pea.
2. Using a pencil, lightly sketch a design on the egg; our pattern is on page 95 or devise a design of your own.
3. Put a folded towel on your worktable and place the egg on it.
4. To pierce the egg, hold a tapestry needle in one hand, point-down and perpendicular to the surface, and gently tap the eye end of the needle with the hammer. Perforate the egg at intervals along the design lines, making holes first with the larger needle and then with the smaller one.
5. Insert one end of the narrower ribbon in the hole in the top of the egg (insert both ends if you prefer a hanging loop). Secure with glue.
6. Tie the wider ribbon in a bow around the inserted ribbon; cut the tails of the bow on an angle. Add the pin or button (if using a button, glue it on).

tip The more holes there are, the weaker the egg, so be increasingly gentle as you pierce the design. It's a smart idea to practice this technique on a test egg!

pattern templates

Fanciful Flowering Stems (page 84) Enlarge 400% (should be about 8 inches long). For each flower, pierce center dot for stem, then cut on dashed lines.

Posy Party Lights (page 67) Cut on solid line, fold on dashed line.

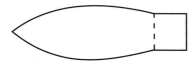 

Strawbunnies (page 43)

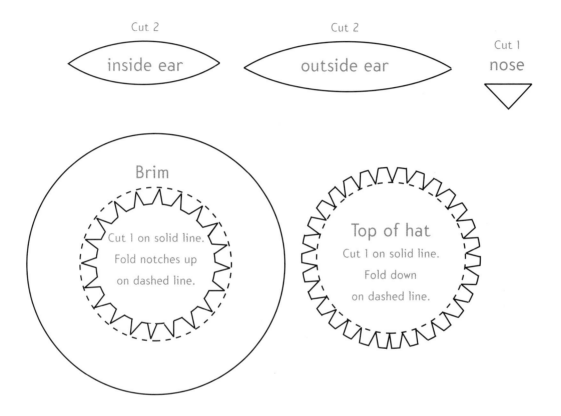

Cut 2

inside ear

Cut 2

outside ear

Cut 1

nose

Brim

Cut 1 on solid line.
Fold notches up
on dashed line.

Top of hat

Cut 1 on solid line.
Fold down
on dashed line.

Side of hat

Cut 1 on solid line.
Form cylinder, overlap at end, and glue.

Tulip Menu Card (page 47)

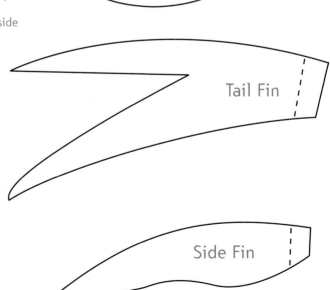

Goldfish Cupcake Toppers (page 87)

For each Cupcake Topper, cut 2 of each side
fin on solid lines. Fold on dotted lines.

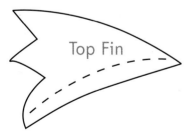

Top Fin

Tail Fin

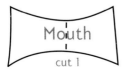

Mouth

cut 1

Side Fin

Good Night-Light (page 64)

Cut out solid details.

Lovely Lacy Egg (page 91)

Piercing pattern: alternate large and small holes.

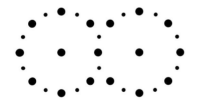

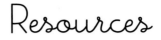
Resources

Most egg-decorating supplies are easily found at your local crafts store. The following online vendors are also excellent—and easy-to-visit—sources.

www.azostrich.com Clean and blown exotic and game-bird eggs, including goose eggs

www.crateandbarrel.com Eggcups, salt wells, other porcelain vessels for perching and displaying eggs

www.dickblick.com Dremel drills and accessories, general art and crafts supplies

www.joann.com Fabrics, glues, craft papers and card stock, moss, Styrofoam forms, paints, beads, and tassels

www.michaels.com Superstore of craft supplies, including ribbons, paints, stickers, sequins, googly eyes, brushes, markers, glitter, candles, craft papers and card stock, and essentials like glue, glue guns, Styrofoam forms, and sewing and cake decorating supplies

www.mms.com Single-colored candies in 12 different shades

www.nhchocolates.com Chocolate bunnies in all shapes, nuts, foil-wrapped eggs, jelly beans, and mixed chocolates. Call 603-225-2591 for out-of-season candies.

www.paaseastereggs.com Egg dyes, tools, and additional instructions for egg dying

www.yummies.com Bagged candies like jelly beans, Jordan almonds, and foil-wrapped eggs

our favorite egg salad

Terrific in sandwiches, this egg salad is equally delicious served in cups of fresh lettuce. Either way, tomatoes and pickles or gherkins are perfect accompaniments. This recipe makes six servings.

gather

For the Egg Salad	For the Mayonnaise
8 eggs	1 egg at room temperature
1 tablespoon white vinegar	1½ tablespoons freshly squeezed lemon juice
⅓ cup mayonnaise, preferably homemade (recipe follows)	½ teaspoon dry mustard
¼ cup diced red onion	Pinch of salt
¼ cup diced celery	Pinch of cayenne
¼ cup canned black olives, pitted and diced	½ cup salad oil
Salt and pepper	

egg salad

1. Let the eggs sit at room temperature for 30 minutes.
2. Bring a saucepan of water to boil. Add the vinegar. Turn heat to low. Gently lower the eggs into the water one at a time, using a slotted spoon. Let simmer for 15 minutes.
3. Drain the eggs and allow to cool. Peel under gently running cold water. Place on a paper towel to dry for a few minutes. You can refrigerate them, covered, at this point for later use.
4. Place eggs in a large mixing bowl. Add mayonnaise, onion, celery, and olives. Mash with a potato masher or fork until well combined. Add salt and pepper to taste. Makes 6 servings.

easy homemade mayonnaise

1. Place the egg, lemon juice, and spices into the jar of a blender. Blend until well combined.
2. With the blender running, add the oil in a slow and steady stream until the mayonnaise is smooth. If it is too thick, add a few more drops of lemon juice. Cover and refrigerate until ready to use. Makes ¾ cup.